Eagles

by Mary K. Dornhoffer
and Robert F. Scherrer

Science Adviser: Terrence E. Young Jr., M.Ed., M.L.S.,
Jefferson Parish (La.) Public Schools

Content Adviser: Jan Jenner, Ph.D.

Reading Adviser: Dr. Linda D. Labbo,
Department of Reading Education, College of Education,
The University of Georgia

COMPASS POINT BOOKS
MINNEAPOLIS, MINNESOTA

FIRST REPORTS

Compass Point Books
3109 West 50th Street, #115
Minneapolis, MN 55410

Visit Compass Point Books on the Internet at *www.compasspointbooks.com*
or e-mail your request to *custserv@compasspointbooks.com*

On the cover: Golden eagle perched on a rock, North America

Photographs ©: Creatas, cover; Richard Day/Daybreak Imagery, 4, 36; Steven Kazlowski/Seapics.com, 5; Stockbyte, 6; Diana L. Stratton/Tom Stack & Associates, 7; Alan G. Nelson/Dembinsky Photo Associates, 8; Anthony Mercieca/Dembinsky Photo Associates, 9, 23; Thomas Kitchin/Tom Stack & Associates, 10, 21; Charles G. Summers/Bruce Coleman Inc., 11; Unicorn Stock Photos/Robert E. Barber, 12–13; Jack Barrie/Bruce Coleman Inc., 14; Joe McDonald, 15, 31, 32; Gary Schultz/Bruce Coleman Inc., 16; Peter Davey/Bruce Coleman Inc., 17; Carlos Sanz—V&W/Bruce Coleman Inc., 18, 29; DigitalVision, 19, 43; Stan Osolinski/Dembinsky Photo Associates, 20, 22; David Ellis/Bruce Coleman Inc., 24–25; Dominique Braud/Dembinsky Photo Associates, 26; Dave Watts/Tom Stack & Associates, 27; AFP/Corbis, 34; U.S. Fish & Wildlife Service/photo by Megan Durham, 35; Digital Stock, 38–39; Photo Network/Mark Sherman, 40–41; Kenneth W. Fink/Bruce Coleman Inc., 42.

Editor: Patricia Stockland
Photo Researcher: Svetlana Zhurkina
Designer/Page Production: Bradfordesign, Inc./Jaime Martens
Cartographer: XNR Productions, Inc.

Library of Congress Cataloging-in-Publication Data
Dornhoffer, Mary K.
    Eagles / by Mary K. Dornhoffer and Robert F. Scherrer.
        p. cm. — (First reports)
    Includes bibliographical references and index.
    ISBN 0-7565-0577-1
    1. Eagles—Juvenile literature. [1. Eagles.] I. Scherrer, Robert F. II. Title. III. Series.
    QL696.F32D68 2004
    598.9'42—dc22   2003014422

Table of Contents

*NOTE: In this book, words that are defined in the glossary are in **bold** the first time they appear in the text.*

Masters of the Sky

▲ *A bald eagle rests in a pine tree.*

The eagle swoops and rides the air currents. Its sharp eyes can see a rabbit 2 miles (3.2 kilometers) away. That's five times sharper than your eyes. Its large wings help it fly fast. When it dives, the eagle can move at almost 200 miles (320 km) per hour. That's faster than a speeding car or train. Majestic and powerful, the eagle is the master of the sky.

▲ *An eagle rides the air currents while searching for food.*

What Do Eagles Look Like?

An eagle is a bird. It has a long head covered with feathers. This is one way to tell the difference between an eagle and a vulture, another large bird that flies very high. A vulture has no feathers on its head.

Eagles have large eyes. Some are the size of a human's eyes or larger. Eagles cannot move their eyes back and forth or up and down like you can. Instead, an eagle can move its neck much farther— in nearly a full circle. In this way, an eagle can see all around.

▲ Unlike a vulture, this bald eagle's head is covered with feathers.

▲ *Golden eagles live in open spaces, such as the plains of Montana.*

An eagle has very long, wide wings. Eagles that live in open spaces have longer wings than eagles that live in forests. Forest eagles have longer tails. The shorter wings and longer tails of forest eagles help them fly through all the trees.

An eagle has a large, hooked beak. It needs this to tear up its food. An eagle's feet are made for grabbing **prey.** An eagle's foot has three toes in front and one in back. Each toe has a talon at the end. This is a long, sharp claw.

▲ *A golden eagle's talons*

Eagles vary in size. The smallest eagle, the Australian little eagle, weighs 1 pound (0.45 kilograms) and has a **wingspan** of 3 feet (90 centimeters). The largest eagle is the harpy eagle. It has a wingspan of 8 feet (2.4 meters) and weighs about 20 pounds (9 kg).

▲ *A harpy eagle grasps its prey.*

Where Do Eagles Live?

Eagles live in every area of the world except Antarctica and New Zealand. Eagles live wherever they can find food to eat. Some eagles live near

▲ *A tawny eagle in Serengeti National Park, Tanzania*

water, and others live in deserts. Some live on prairies, and some live in forests. Some eagles even live around high mountains. Many eagles will migrate to warmer areas if a harsh winter makes it hard to find food.

Eagles live in nests called eyries.

▲ *The eyries of bald eagles are often as large as a human's bed, and sometimes much larger.*

Eagles live together in pairs, with their babies, in the eyrie. The eyrie is made out of anything the eagles can find, such as sticks, grass, and mud. The eyrie may be high on a cliff or in a tree. Most eagles use the same nest year

▲ *A bald eagle nest high on a cliff*

after year, adding to it each year. If an eagle pair dies, another pair may move into the nest. Some nests are more than 100 years old and very large. A bald eagle nest in Ohio was 20 feet (6 m) high and more than 9 feet (2.7 m) wide. It weighed about 3 tons (2,700 kg)! It was so heavy that it collapsed the tree that was holding it.

How Do Eagles Fly?

An eagle's wings, feathers, and bones were made for flying. Like other birds, eagles have hollow bones. These make the eagle's body very light, so it can get off the ground and fly very high. The feathers of an eagle are also very light. They overlap to make a very

▲ *Overlapping feathers help trap air that lifts an eagle in flight.*

▲ *A bald eagle has more than 7,000 feathers.*

strong wing. The wide, long shape of an eagle's wing helps the eagle to glide in the air without a lot of work. Eagles don't always need to flap their wings to fly. An eagle will use its wide wings to float on a rising current of hot air, called a thermal. These currents occur everywhere, even during winter.

▲ *An eagle can rise and glide on a thermal without flapping its wings.*

What Do Eagles Eat?

▲ *A martial eagle sits with its prey.*

Different kinds of eagles eat different kinds of food. Eagles are top predators. This means that other animals rarely eat eagles. Eagles eat rabbits, prairie dogs, and squirrels. Some eagles eat very large animals, such as small antelope and deer. They also eat insects, fish, snakes, and other birds, including sparrows, ducks, and turkeys. Eagles will eat almost anything they can catch. They will even steal prey from other birds or eagles.

Eagles also eat carrion, which is dead prey. Carrion is an important food source for eagles that live in colder areas—especially during winter, when it is harder to find live prey.

▲ *A royal eagle attacks a wild boar piglet.*

How Do Eagles Hunt?

▲ *An African fish eagle in flight*

An eagle's body is well suited for hunting. The eagle uses its sharp eyes to find prey. Many eagles will watch for prey from a high perch. If there are no trees for perching, an eagle will fly over an area until it spots something to eat.

▲ *This tawny eagle hunts from a treetop in Masai Mara National Reserve, Kenya.*

The eagle uses its powerful wings to quickly swoop down on its prey. It can catch a fish right out of the water. Some eagles will dive into the water to catch big fish.

The eagle uses its feet and talons to grab its prey. The foot can close around the prey just like a fist. The eagle then stabs the prey with its back talon.

Eagles are such good hunters that they do not have to spend much time looking for food. If an eagle captures something big enough, it won't have to hunt for several days.

▲ *A bald eagle holds a freshly caught fish in its talons.*

Eagle Families

▲ *Eagle pairs stay mates for life.*

An eagle finds a mate when it is about 4 years old. The male eagle courts the female eagle with flying **acrobatics.** These special air shows are called courtship flights.

An eagle pair will stay together their entire lives. They work together to build their nest, so the female eagle can lay her eggs.

The mother eagle usually lays two eggs. She keeps the eggs warm by sitting on them until they hatch. This takes about 35 days. Sometimes the father eagle will sit on the eggs, so the mother can get something to eat.

▲ *Golden eagle eggs in a nest*

▲ *This young golden eagle may kill its sibling after it hatches.*

The baby eagle, called an eaglet, hatches out of its egg by pecking on the shell with its egg tooth. This is a hard knob on the end of its beak.

Usually only one eaglet will survive. Unlike other birds that wait for a whole **clutch** to be laid, mother eagles begin to **incubate** each egg as it is laid. Therefore, the first egg laid is usually the first to hatch. The first eaglet to hatch will often kill the second eaglet to hatch. It does this by pushing it from the nest, pecking it, or taking all its food. Scientists do not know why eagles do this.

An eaglet grows very quickly. By the time it is 3 months old, it will be as big as its parents and learning how to fly. It will stay around the nest for a little while longer, so it can improve its flying and learn how to hunt. During this time, the parents feed the eaglet.

By the time the eaglet is about 5 months old, it will be on its own. Most eagles do not reach full adulthood until their third or fourth year, though.

▲ *A 4-week-old bald eagle*

Types of Eagles

▲ *A white-bellied sea eagle feeds its 3-week-old eaglet.*

Eagles are part of the bird family. They belong to a special group of birds called raptors. This means birds of prey—they hunt their food while flying. Other members of this group include falcons, harriers, kites, hawks, and European vultures.

There are 59 different kinds, or species, of eagles. They belong to four different groups. The members of each group all have something in common, such as the shape of their bodies or the type of food they eat.

The first group is the fish or sea eagle group. Fish eagles live on the shores of lakes, rivers, and oceans. They live near warm tropical waters, except for South America, and as far north as the Arctic Circle. Fish eagles swoop down on fish that swim near the surface of the water. They also float down over their prey as if they were wearing a parachute. Fish eagles have rough bumps on the bottom of their toes that help them hold on to fish. The bald eagle and the Steller's sea eagle, the third largest of all the eagles, are in this group.

The second group of eagles is the snake eagle group. They are also called serpent eagles. Snake eagles live in the grasslands and forests of Europe,

▲ Snake eagles are protected from snake bites by many feathers.

Asia, Australia, and Africa. Snake eagles eat all kinds of snakes, except for big ones like boa constrictors and pythons. These eagles have short, strong toes for holding on to their wiggling prey. Snake eagles will also eat lizards and frogs. They can even eat **venomous** snakes, such as cobras. Their thick feathers protect them from snakebites. When a snake strikes a snake eagle, the snake gets a mouthful of feathers.

The African bateleur is a snake eagle. Bateleur is the French word for **acrobat.** The African bateleur has a very short tail, so it uses its wings to control its flight. This makes it fly with a rocking motion that looks like it is doing acrobatics. Barely flapping its wings, it can often soar for hours and is capable of doing complete rolls.

The third eagle group is the booted eagle group. Booted eagles are also called true eagles. They have feathers on their legs all the way down

▲ *This brightly-colored African bateleur eagle is part of the snake eagle group.*

▲ *The African martial eagle belongs to the booted eagle group, also known as true eagles.*

to their feet. They look like they are wearing boots. Many different types of booted eagles exist, including the golden eagle of North America, Europe, and Asia, the wedge-tailed eagle of Australia, and the African martial eagle.

Harpy eagles make up the fourth group of eagles. These eagles live in the tropical forests of South America, New Guinea, Mexico, the Philippines, and Africa. Harpy eagles are all very large. They eat animals such as tree sloths and monkeys. The harpy eagle of South America is the largest eagle in the world. The second-largest eagle in the world is the Philippine eagle. It used to be called the Philippine monkey-eating eagle. Actually, it eats more **flying lemurs** than monkeys, so it was renamed.

Where to See Eagles

People can see eagles in zoos. Many eagles are in zoos because they have been injured and cannot live safely in the wild. To see eagles in the wild, people can go on eagle tours. These are held at parks and eagle reserves when eagles are migrating.

▲ *The Philippine eagle is endangered.*

Eagles in Danger

▲ *A trained wildlife officer is a good source of information about eagles and other raptors.*

Eagles have been misunderstood and killed by people. In the past, groups of people such as ranchers and chicken farmers tried to get rid of golden eagles

▲ *Golden eagles, often hunted in the past by farmers and ranchers, feed on a deer carcass.*

and bald eagles. They thought these eagles were eating their chickens, lambs, and other livestock. Eagles in the western United States were hunted from airplanes, and people were given rewards for killing eagles. Because of this, these eagles almost became extinct. It was finally shown that eagles ate very few lambs and chickens.

Eagles are large animals, so they need large places to live and hunt. When people construct buildings and houses in forests, prairies, and lake areas, eagles are forced to find other places to live. If eagles have nowhere else to live, they might die.

Eagles have also been killed by human-made items, such as power lines and insecticides, or insect poisons. The insecticide DDT nearly caused the bald eagle to become extinct. DDT was eaten by insects, which were eaten by smaller birds or fish. The eagles that ate these birds or fish got a lot of DDT in every meal. This caused the female eagles to lay eggs with soft shells. The eggs all broke when the mother eagle sat on them. In 1972, DDT was banned in the United States. Other countries also banned it.

People no longer fear or hunt eagles. They are respected as strong and beautiful creatures. Now, the population of the bald eagle, the national symbol of the United States, has been steadily increasing.

▲ *The bald eagle almost became extinct. Its population is now increasing.*

Protecting Eagles

▲ *A wildlife officer holding a young bald eagle*

Other steps are being taken to protect eagles. In the United States, it is against the law to kill or capture an eagle. You cannot even own an eagle feather unless

you belong to a Native American tribe. The nests of the very endangered Philippine eagles are protected from poachers by armed guards.

Many eagles are being raised in captivity and reintroduced to the wild. Nesting areas are being protected, and land is being set aside for eagles and other raptors. Money is being spent to bury power lines and to build nesting platforms on towers.

People are learning what hurts eagles. They are doing things to protect them.

Special events are held to teach the public more about eagles' environments. Some people take tours to watch eagles migrate, nest, or hunt. Some groups even take care of eagles that have been orphaned or disabled.

With continued education and effort, we will always be able to enjoy these masters of the sky.

▲ *The magnificent harpy eagle*

▲ *African fish eagles*

Glossary

acrobat—someone who skillfully performs gymnastic exercises

acrobatics—the artistic demonstration and act of an acrobat

clutch—a group of eggs or chicks

flying lemurs—a nocturnal animal about the size of a cat that can leap long distances, which appears as flying

incubate—to keep eggs warm so that they will hatch

prey—an animal hunted by another animal for food

wingspan—the distance from wingtip to wingtip

venomous—something containing venom, a poisonous matter or substance

Did You Know?

- A bald eagle does not get its white head until it is about 5 years old.

- The foot of the harpy eagle is 10 inches (25.4 cm) long, and its talons can be 5 inches (12.7 cm) long.

- Eagles use just about anything to build their nests, including old shoes and bottles.

- In the wild, eagles may live to be 20 years old.

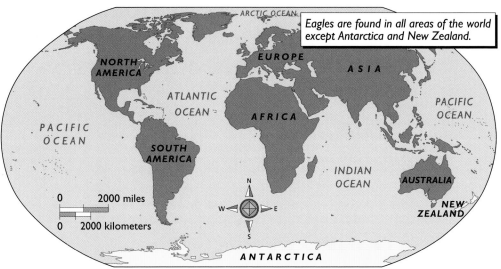

Eagles are found in all areas of the world except Antarctica and New Zealand.

Range: Eagles live in every area of the world except for Antarctica and New Zealand. They live in forests, prairies, and deserts, on mountains, and near water.

Species: There are 59 species of eagles.

Size: The smallest eagle, the Australian little eagle, weighs 1 pound (0.45 kg) and has a wingspan of 3 feet (90 cm). The largest eagle is the harpy eagle. It weighs about 20 pounds (9 kg) and has a wingspan of 8 feet (2.4 m).

Diet: Eagles eat large animals, such as antelope and deer, and smaller animals, such as rabbits, prairie dogs, and squirrels. Eagles will also eat insects, fish, and other birds.

Young: Eaglets hatch from an egg. The mother eagle usually lays two eggs.

Want to Know More?

At the Library

Gieck, Charlene. *Eagles for Kids*. Minocqua, Wis.: NorthWord
    Press, 1991.

Grambo, Rebecca L. *Eagles, Masters of the Sky*. St. Paul: Voyageur
    Press, 1997.

Hodge, Deborah. Illustrated by Nancy Gray Ogle. *Eagles*. Toronto:
    Kids Can Press, 2000.

On the Web

For more information on eagles, use FactHound
to track down Web sites related to this book.

    1. Go to *www.compasspointbooks.com/facthound*
    2. Type in this book ID: 0756505771
    3. Click on the *Fetch It* button.

Your trusty FactHound will fetch the best Web sites for you!

Through the Mail

The Raptor Center at Auburn University

1350 Raptor Road
Auburn, AL 36849-5523
334/844-6025
For more information about the oldest raptor rehabilitation
center in the southeastern United States

On the Road

Pinnacle Mountain State Park

11901 Pinnacle Valley Road
Roland, AR 72135
501/868-5806
To view wintering bald eagles

About the Authors

Mary K. Dornhoffer holds a degree in chemistry and a minor in English and has been a scientific writer for the past 17 years. In addition to authoring technical manuals, scientific proposals, and children's books, she is a published poet. She lives near Little Rock, Arkansas, with her husband, John, and her two boys, Tommy and Jimmy.

Robert Scherrer's career has been in computer science and information systems. He has also pursued numerous activities based on his lifelong interest in animals. Presently, he volunteers at the St. Louis Zoo, where he does animal observation for the zoo's research group. He lives in St. Louis, Missouri, with his wife, Joan.